MASTERING
EXPLAINED

BY MICHAEL COSTA AND CHAD JOHNSON

CONTENTS

To access video visit:
www.halleonard.com/mylibrary

"Enter Code"
8102-9906-1771-6929

ISBN 978-1-5400-5949-9

HAL•LEONARD®

Visit Hal Leonard Online at
www.halleonard.com

Contact us:
Hal Leonard
7777 West Bluemound Road
Milwaukee, WI 53213
Email: info@halleonard.com

In Europe, contact:
Hal Leonard Europe Limited
42 Wigmore Street
Marylebone, London, W1U 2RN
Email: info@halleonardeurope.com

In Australia, contact:
Hal Leonard Australia Pty. Ltd.
4 Lentara Court
Cheltenham, Victoria, 3192 Australia
Email: info@halleonard.com.au

INTRODUCTION

Mastering is one of the most critical steps in music production. It's often what sets apart a mix that sounds merely "good" from one that sounds "professional" or "radio-ready." Yet, it's also been one of the most mysterious and least-understood practices of all. Indeed, many people don't have an accurate idea what a mastering engineer does, much less how he/she does it. It's seemingly been a closely guarded secret for decades, with the magical formula only revealed to a precious few. In recent times, however, as the playing field continues to be leveled more and more regarding recording equipment, software, and the like, the veil is slowly being lifted from this mystical art. Finally, aided with this newly shared knowledge—along with plugin versions of the necessary sonic tools—we commoners are beginning to achieve professional-sounding results that can begin to hold their own when stacked up against the big boys.

Enter *Mastering Explained*. In this book, we'll break down the many layers of the mastering process and dissect each one, explaining the why and how in detail. It's important to realize that mastering, much like mixing—and playing a musical instrument or writing a song, for that matter—is an art just as much as it is a science, and therefore it will take some time and practice to develop your skills. Every song or album is different, and likewise, every mastering task is different. While there are many common processes used from one project to the next, there's no "set it and forget it" formula that can be applied to every song. Each track will present its own strengths and weaknesses and will require a unique approach, just as is the case when mixing a song.

While many mastering houses will make use of expensive dedicated outboard gear (EQs, compressors, limiters, etc.), it's safe to say that most people recording at home or in a modest studio won't have access to those elite pieces. Therefore, this book—as well as the accompanying videos—will focus entirely on using "in the box" software plugins to achieve similar sonic results. Sure, Pultec EQs and SSL buss compressors certainly are nice pieces of gear, but the aim of this book is not to force you to take out a second mortgage on your home. You'll be relieved to know that the plugins referenced in this book can be had for hundreds of dollars at most (and some much cheaper), as opposed to thousands at least!

Again, although this book will detail the tools and techniques commonly used in the mastering process, it can't master a song for you. It's important to remember that the art of mastering takes practice. Granted, we can promise that your tracks should certainly sound markedly improved on most fronts after working through this book/video package, but it will likely still take time and experience before you'll be happy comparing your tracks side by side with the top dogs. It's the old 80/20 adage—you'll probably spend 20% of your time getting 80% there, but you'll spend 80% of your time getting the remaining 20% of the way. Don't worry—you can get there if you keep at it!

ABOUT THE VIDEOS

Throughout the book, video icons ▶ will signal you when a video exists pertaining to a certain topic. You can access these videos by going to www.halleonard.com/mylibrary and entering the code you find toward the bottom of page 1 (the title page) in this book. (Look for the box that says "Enter Code.")

We all know the expression "a picture is worth a thousand words." To a musician, we can recast that as "an audio example is worth a thousand words." You'll get plenty of those in the accompanying videos. In fact, you get even better—you'll have access to audio *and* video. So not only do you get to *hear* the concepts from the book being applied in real examples, you get to *see* the process—the virtual knob-tweaking, as it were—as well.

Some folks are more visual learners, while others prefer the written word. But regardless of which side of this line you fall on, it's imperative that you check out the videos in order to get the most out of this method. After all, music is an auditory art, and there's simply no substitute for hearing the effect of these tools on actual music.

Virtually all of the topics covered in this book are addressed with their own videos, and the most comprehensive understanding of these concepts can be achieved by combining the written and video resources. While the text may expand more on certain topics than the videos will, the videos will obviously "say" more at times with one 10-second demonstration than the text can in five pages. That's not to discount the text element, but rather to say that each element has its strength. You'd be well-advised to study both if you want to achieve the deepest level of understanding with this material.

CHAPTER 1
THE BASICS

WHAT IS MASTERING? ▶

Before we get to the nitty gritty—or even just the nitty—let's first talk about what mastering exactly is and why we do it. This actually isn't a simple question, because mastering can mean not only different things to different people, but it can also mean a different thing to the same person when working on different projects. Nevertheless, there are several elements of the mastering that occur within the process more often than not.

Now, major labels—and even many indie labels—have a simple solution for this part of the process: they simply send their mixes to a top-grade mastering house for a professional job. This is figured as part of their costs in producing an album (or single), so it's factored into their budget from the start. This is done for numerous reasons, such as:

- **It's what they do:** A professional mastering engineer has honed their craft over years of practice, specifically concentrating on the art of mastering. Therefore, they think and hear like a mastering engineer by default. (This is something we'll talk more about later.)
- **Top-notch facilities:** A mastering house will no-doubt have acoustically designed rooms that are tailor-made with audio production in mind. This is simply not an option for most home-recording enthusiasts, so we're forced to work with what we have.
- **Serious toys:** Along with a stellar room, a professional mastering house will have gear—*lots* of it. Not only that, but it will most likely be top-shelf and dedicated to the mastering process. This may include plugins, but (in true pro mastering houses) it will also surely include costly outboard gear that's firmly planted in the "stuff of dreams" category for the rest of us. They often spare no expense when it comes to the converters (Digital-to-Analog and vice versa) as well.
- **Objectivity:** A professional mastering engineer will be hearing these mixes for the first time and will therefore bring a welcome level of objectivity to the process that's hard to achieve on our own.

Of course, if you're reading this book, then it's most likely because you don't have the same budget as these major labels. Don't worry—you're not alone! The digital recording revolution has placed countless others in the same boat. That's where this book/video package comes in. Our aim is to help you achieve similar results within the confines of your home studio.

So, again, what does a mastering engineer do exactly? Typically, the job of a mastering engineer may involve any or every one of the following:

- Increasing the loudness (or perceived loudness) of a song or group of songs
- Trimming the beginnings/ends and/or adding fade-ins or fade-outs to the songs
- Matching the timbre (brightness/darkness, etc.) and loudness of a series of songs so they balance well together on an album or EP
- Addressing broad problem areas in a mix, such as excessive high end, boomy bass, or more specific instrument-related issues
- Adding a professional sheen or clarity to a previously dull-sounding mix
- Arranging the songs of an album in a specific order and adding the appropriate space between each song
- Delivering files specifically tailored for a particular medium (CD, radio, film, digital, etc.)

Again, each project is different, so there's no "one-size-fits-all" solution when it comes to mastering. There's no magic button labeled "professional sound" that the pros simply push once and call it done.

So, before we start twisting knobs, let's address a few preliminary topics that will greatly affect the approach we need to take.

SINGLE TRACKS VS. A COLLECTION OF TRACKS ▶

With the advent of digital music stores like iTunes and Amazon Music, it's become quite commonplace for people to purchase one song at a time. Therefore, due to the law of supply and demand, it's become customary for bands or artists to release one song at a time as well. This means that the song would be mastered in isolation, without worrying about how it sits next to other songs. In this instance, your job as a mastering engineer is a bit easier because all you need to worry about is getting that particular song to sound the best you can.

However, things get more complicated as soon as you add another song to the tally, especially in the case of several songs that are meant to be released together (like an album or EP). This is because you now must worry about how those songs sound together as opposed to in isolation. You may be dealing with songs that were recorded in entirely different studios with wholly different equipment. Or it could be several songs that were recorded years apart from each other with substantially different sounds or sonic character. All of these variables could result in a more complicated mastering process. We'll talk about these specific types of challenges as we progress through the book.

One of the goals we'll strive for in this regard is addressed in what is called the "couch test." Simply put, if you start the album and adjust the volume of the first track to a comfortable level, then you should be able to sit on the couch and listen to the recording in its entirety without feeling the need to make any adjustments—be it volume, EQ, or otherwise. That's one of our goals when mastering a collection of songs.

Keep in mind that this may mean compromising some aspects of a track for the good of the whole project. For example, if you're mastering a compilation of pre-released tracks, and they're all over the place regarding loudness, then you may have to turn down the louder tracks for the lower-volume ones to compete. After all, you can only turn up a track so much before you start hearing distortion. If the quieter tracks can't reach the level of the louder ones without introducing some unwanted artifacts, then your only option is to bring the volume level of the louder tracks down to that of the quieter ones. Similarly, it may mean slightly dulling down some tracks to compensate for ones that significantly lack sheen (especially if brightening them up causes consequent damage).

It may be helpful to think of an analogy in the mixing process. A common beginner's mistake when mixing is to solo each track and apply EQ until each one sounds great. Of course, what you soon realize is that it's not important how each instrument sounds in isolation, because that's not the way they're going to be heard. The important thing is how they sound within the entire mix.

The same can be said for mastering a collection of songs. If Track 1 sounds amazing with crisp, clear highs, but Track 2 doesn't sound that way, then you'll most likely need to compromise. Track 1 will need to "take one for the team," as it were, and possibly dull some of its sheen in order to make the whole album sound more consistent and cohesive when listening from beginning to end.

MASTERING YOUR WORK VS. SOMEONE ELSE'S ▶

Another extremely important concept to consider is whose work you are mastering. If you're mastering somebody else's album or song, then you get the benefit of objectivity and a fresh ear. This is a great exercise—as is mixing someone else's track(s). We highly recommend you give it a go at some point, if for no other reason than the experience that comes with it. It's quite eye-opening to place yourself in someone else's project and hear things through their perspective. You can learn a lot—both things you like and things you don't like—and you'll certainly become a better mastering engineer for it.

However, many people reading this book are most likely going to try their hand at mastering their own material. And while this book is largely dedicated to this idea, there are a few things to keep in mind in this regard:

- **Loss of objectivity:** As the saying goes, "Two heads are better than one." If you're mastering a song that you mixed yourself, then you're likely not going to hear many problem areas; otherwise, you would have addressed them during the mixing process.

- **Reinforcement of acoustical issues:** If you master a song in the same room that you mixed in, then you'll be dealing with the same problems that occurred during the mixing process. In other words, if there's an excessive bass build-up at your mixing position, then you'll likely be turning down the bass during the mixing process to counter that. If you were to send that mix to someone else for mastering, they would likely hear that lack of bass in your mix and compensate for it (as best they can) in the mastering process. But if you're in the same room, then you're most likely not going to hear that.

There are two main ways to combat these issues. Let's look at them one by one.

TIME

Although we can say things like, "You have to think like a mastering engineer," or, "Try to imagine you're hearing the song as a first-time listener," the truth is that it's very hard to get outside your own headspace. To this end, objectivity with your own work is a significant hurdle. The best solution in this regard is to give it time. If possible, try to wait a few months between the mixing and mastering stages. You've no doubt listened to these songs countless times during the mixing process. The worst thing you can do—if you want to remain objective at all—is immediately turn around and attempt to master them. If you do this, then you're sure to not notice any problem areas—things that may immediately jump out had you waited a few months.

The ear is extremely good at acclimating to sound. For example, you can hear something and immediately think it sounds very boomy. But if you give it a few minutes, you'll most likely acclimate to it and won't notice it anymore. This issue, known as **ear fatigue**, is why it's so important to take breaks during the mixing process. And the same goes for the mastering process. Therefore, after you've mixed the album/EP, try to wait for a month or more—without listening to the tracks at all—before beginning to master the recordings. This will give you the best shot at being objective when hearing the tracks again.

REFERENCE MATERIAL AND MULTIPLE LISTENING DEVICES

You can do your very best to treat any acoustical problems in your control room, such as installing sound absorption materials, bass traps, diffusers, etc. However, chances are, unless you built the room from the ground up with music production in mind, you'll likely be dealing with a less-than-ideal situation. One of your best allies in combating problem areas in your room is to compare your tracks to reference material on multiple systems. Of course, this is beneficial during mixing as well, but it's sometimes overlooked in the mastering realm despite its merits.

Listen to your track, and compare it to a professional recording that's similar in style and instrumentation, etc. How bright is the pro track compared to yours? How much bass is present? How prominent is the mid-range? Do the same thing on at least three different listening systems. Aside from your studio monitors (if you only have one set), also listen through a few sets of headphones (studio headphones, earbuds, etc.), a Bluetooth speaker, a TV, or a clock radio with an auxiliary input jack, etc. The more comparisons you can make on different systems, the more chances you'll have at combating the issues in your room. Make notes of what you hear on each system, and adjust the track in the spirit of compromise, trying your best to achieve a sound that's palatable between all the systems.

"Mastering" an Album Song-by-Song During the Mixing Process?

Some people say that they don't feel they need a mastering engineer because they're essentially making the song sound "radio-ready" during the mixing process. For example, they may have the mix where they want it and then apply some compression (for "glue") and EQ across the mixing buss, as well as a brick wall limiter to raise the overall level of the track to where they want. And they may call that a done deal and then move on to the next song.

Now, since music is a subjective art, there's no way whether to say that these people have or haven't "mastered" the song. But the problem with doing this is that you're going to be in the weeds with mixing one song when you begin to "master" it. Aside from the problem of ear fatigue, which we discussed earlier, the issue with this is that you're not considering the album in a bigger picture, as a whole. You're just making each song sound the best on its own without considering the entire project.

Whereas mixing is more "in the trees," mastering is usually more about the forest. And if you essentially master each song while you're mixing it, you're going to be too wrapped up in the trees (that one song) to see the forest (the album in its entirety). This is why it's more beneficial when dealing with a collection of songs to treat the mastering process as a completely separate task (again, preferably at a later date). Most professional mastering is done with stereo mixes only, which means that you shouldn't really be dealing with detailed mix issues anymore. This allows you (or the pro mastering engineer) to get into a different mindset—one in which you're not dealing with surgical tools anymore, but rather with broader strokes. You'll think differently in this situation and be focused on more of the bigger picture by default.

Of course, this isn't to say that you won't ever address specific mix issues. There are times when professional mastering houses will send a song back to the mixing engineer if there's an issue that's too blatant to ignore. And, of course, if you hear such an issue when mastering your own song (after allowing ample time from the mixing to get a fresh perspective, of course), then it's a simple matter to go back and address that issue in the mix before trying the mastering process again.

There are also some techniques we can use when mastering stereo mixes to help address smaller problems, and we'll talk about them in the coming chapters. You may be dealing with an old stereo mix and have no access to the individual tracks anymore. In those instances, you have to work with what you've got.

Having said this, we'll concentrate through most of this book on mastering with a stereo mix. We'll briefly discuss mastering with stems later in the book, but by far, the vast majority of what we do will deal with stereo mixes. I encourage you to take this approach in your own work, as it helps bookend the mixing and mastering processes, which enables you to think of the album more as a whole unit, rather than a collection of individual songs.

CHAPTER 2
EQ, DYNAMICS, AND DITHER

Now that we have a better idea of what we mean by the term "mastering," let's get down to business. In this chapter, we're going to look at two of the most common sonic tools in the mastering engineer's arsenal: **EQ** and **compression**. These two effects, which essentially control tone (or timbre) and dynamics, respectively, make up a great deal of what mastering fundamentally is, so it's crucial that you have a thorough understanding of how to use each tool. We'll also address the lesser-discussed concept of **dither** and why it's important.

EQ

The primary way we control the tone of a track—i.e., brightness, dullness, presence, bass, treble, etc.—is with equalization, or EQ. If you've spent any time mixing your music (or someone else's), you've no doubt dealt with this tool extensively. However, while we may use similar tools in this regard when mastering as we do when mixing, the way we use them is usually a bit different.

First of all, we need to think big picture when mastering. This usually means using broad strokes rather than surgical cuts. In other words, while it's very common to dial in a narrow bandwidth frequency on a certain instrument for enhancement or reduction during mixing, it's more prevalent in mastering to use gentle shelving or wide-band shallow peaks (or dips). This is because when a song reaches the mastering stage, it should ideally be rid of any harsh peaks or incredibly boomy bass sounds, etc. If the song has been mixed well, then it will usually only need some gentle therapy regarding EQ, as opposed to a complete overhaul.

Also, keep in mind that the decibel (dB) values used are generally much less aggressive when mastering than when mixing. Whereas 8 or 10 dB boost/cuts may not seem out of place during the mixing stage, these types of values are practically unheard of when mastering. During the mastering process, a boost or cut of 3 dB is considered quite large, with values of 1 to 2 dB generally being more common. Again, we're generally thinking of subtle tonal therapy rather than full-on reconstructive surgery, as may be necessary when mixing.

EQ TOOLBOX
So let's take a quick look at the types of EQ tools we'll be using during our mastering sessions. Generally speaking, they're not too different from those we use while mixing. Even though we talked about using broad strokes, it's still important to have fine control over where those broad strokes lie, so a solid multi-band parametric EQ is a nice place to start. Depending on your particular **Digital Audio Workstation (DAW)**, you may have some included plugins that will nicely do the trick. Otherwise, there are plenty of options available in various price ranges, such as IK Multimedia's T-RackS Master EQ 432 and Waves' Linear Phase EQ.

T-RackS Master EQ 432   Waves Linear Phase EQ

Generally speaking, you'll want to use the most transparent EQ you have when mastering. The idea behind this is that you've most likely added "coloration" during the mixing process and therefore won't need to do so during mastering. There are some exceptions to this. For example, if you're mastering very old material and only have access to the stereo mix file, then you may want to add an additional dimension by using a more colorful EQ (or other processors).

It may also be the case that you find one track sticks out much more than the others when mastering a group of songs. This could be because it was possibly recorded at a different time or location and/or with different equipment, etc. In these cases, a colorful EQ may be just what the track needs. We'll talk more about this idea later. All things being equal, though, it's safe to say that a transparent EQ is a good place to start.

EQ TECHNIQUES

As mentioned earlier, the mastering process generally makes use of larger brush strokes regarding EQ. This is because we shouldn't be dealing with big problem areas at this point—those areas should have (ideally) been addressed during the mixing stage. Instead, we're usually just massaging the audio slightly, giving it gentle nudges that help create the final polish that it needs. In other words, if mixing is the sanding stage of a woodworking project, mastering is the clear coat and polish.

Don't Forget to Compare!

When making EQ adjustments—or any adjustments for that matter—be sure to bypass the plugin occasionally so you can compare what you're doing to the unaffected track. This will help ensure that you're moving along correctly and aren't doing more damage than good!

Shelving

When it comes to this use of broad strokes in mastering, **shelving** is a popular EQ technique. In case you're not familiar with how shelving works, it involves the boosting or cutting of all frequencies above or below a specific point. In terms of mastering, we're usually dealing with much smaller boosts or cuts than when in the mixing stage. As was mentioned before, a boost/cut of 3 dB is considered quite large in the mastering process:

High shelf boost at 5 kHz *Low shelf cut at 125 Hz*

One of the most common uses for shelving is to provide a bit more high end to a song that slightly sounds dull. Depending on the track, the frequency of the shelf could be anywhere from 2 kHz up to 10 kHz or higher. If it only seems to be missing that "top end sheen," then start around 10 kHz. But if it also seems dull throughout the upper mid-range as well, then it may be necessary to bring it down as far as the 2 or 3 kHz area:

High shelf boost of 2 dB at 10 kHz *High shelf boost of 1.5 dB at 3 kHz*

Sometimes a track may feel rather lightweight on the bottom end. In this case, a gentle shelving boost in the bass can help give it a bit more impact. Be careful not to place this shelf too high, as muddiness can occur once you start creeping up above the 200 Hz area. You're usually looking for a point from around 50–150 Hz with this type of boost:

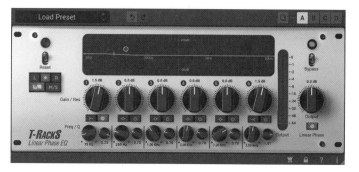

Low shelf boost of 1.5 dB at 75 Hz

Of course, shelving is not just for adding bass or treble frequencies. You can also use it to tame excessive boominess or brightness. If the song's bass and/or kick drum are throbbing a bit too much, for example, then you can use a shelving EQ to make a cut instead of a boost. A recommended strategy here is to start very low (around 40 Hz) and slowly sweep up until you reach the desired amount of cut. You may end up with the cut placed anywhere from 50 or 60 Hz to 150 Hz or higher, depending on the track.

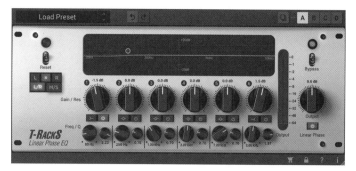

Low shelf cut of 1.5 dB at 80 Hz

Likewise, if the top end is sizzling too much on a track, then try adding a cut on the high-band shelf. Again, start high (20 kHz or so), and slowly sweep down until you find the sweet spot.

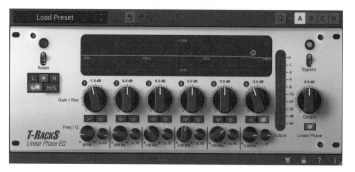

High shelf cut of 2 dB at 12 kHz

What's Too Bright or Too Dull?

So the question arises when talking about these shelving EQ strategies: What's too bright, too dull, too bassy, etc.? This isn't always an easy question to answer because these terms can be subjective, of course. However, it's important to remember what you're trying to achieve at this stage. You're most likely trying to make all the songs on an album sound like a cohesive unit. In this case, "too bright" or "too dull" would be in reference to the other songs that appear on the album.

Of course, you have to start with one song, so how do you know if it's too bright or dull, etc.? That's where **referencing** comes in. Find a professionally mastered track (or tracks) that sounds like the project you're working on. Assuming you like the way it sounds, you can use it as a meter to gauge the brightness/dullness of your track(s). Once you get your own track in the ballpark, then you can work to make them all sound similar.

Of course, if you're simply mastering one track (a single, for instance), then you only need to make use of some professional reference tracks and do the best you can with that one song. Again, it helps to use songs that sound similar to yours in style and timbre.

Refocusing

Another EQ strategy is **refocusing**. For this, we use a normal (bell curve) band as opposed to a shelf. This means we'll have three adjustable variables: the frequency, the amount of boost or cut, and the bandwidth or "Q." The purpose of refocusing is to create a small illusion in a track that suffers from any type of excessive trait, such as boominess, shrillness, dullness, etc. The idea is that, after applying some shelving EQ to address the main issue, we can sweep to find a pleasant frequency within the track that helps slightly refocus the ear away from the problem area. This works in conjunction with the shelving EQ to create a more balanced tone overall.

For example, if we have a track that's excessively dull, then we may apply a shelf at around 3 kHz on the top band to slightly brighten it. But then with the next band, we can search for a frequency that sounds pleasant and gives it a gentle boost to help reshape the sound picture. You'll need to use your ears for this to sweep up and down to find it, as it will be different in every track. It helps to exaggerate the amount of boost at first—maybe around 5 or 6 dB, which is huge in the mastering stage—to more quickly identify the area, knowing that you'll be backing the boost off once you've settled on the appropriate frequency.

So let's say that we locate about 3.5 kHz as a nice frequency to boost. We'd lower the amount down to a more reasonable number, such as 2.5 dB or so, and use a relatively wide bandwidth. In other words, the Q would likely be 1 dB or higher, since we're not looking for a surgical boost here. We want a gentle rolling hill—not a drastic spike. So we'd end up with something like this:

High shelf boost plus refocus boost of
2.5 dB at 3.5 kHz

The same idea can be applied to the low end as well. If you have a track that's too thin on the bottom, then you can apply this two-step EQ method to help give it more weight while also adding a bit of punch. The process would be the same. Start by adding a shelf to thicken the low end, and then use the next band to sweep to for a pleasant frequency that can provide a slight amount of punch. You may also want to find a spot that accentuates the kick drum or the bass guitar, etc. The idea is to find a spot that sounds pleasant when you give it a little boost but doesn't draw too much attention to itself.

Low shelf boost plus refocus boost of
1.5 dB at 80 Hz

We can make use of EQ in other ways at times during the mastering process, but these two methods will likely constitute the bulk of the duties. We'll talk about some other more specific EQ solutions later when we deal with some problem tracks.

DYNAMICS ▶

Apart from equalization, which mostly deals with the balance of tone and timbre, the other large part of mastering centers around **dynamics**, which deals mostly with the balance of volume levels. The tools used for this are **compression** and **limiting**. We use various types of these effects in the mastering process, some of which are also applied during tracking and/or mixing. Other types are generally more common during mastering.

Compression/limiting is perhaps debated more than most effects when it comes to whether or not it should be applied at various stages throughout a song. For instance, some swear by using it when tracking certain instruments, while others insist that you should wait until the mixing stage to apply it. Some like to apply compression across the stereo buss while mixing, while others prefer to leave that to the mastering stage. Some of these issues could depend upon the resources you have available—if you only have one favorite outboard compressor, for example, then you can't very well wait until the mix to apply it to more than one track. Many times, it's simply a matter of your own taste and/or preferred workflow.

In this section, we'll focus mostly on **buss compressors** and **peak (brickwall) limiters**. We'll look at other types of compression (and compressors/limiters) in later chapters.

BUSS COMPRESSION TOOLBOX

When we say **buss compression**, we're referring to using a single compressor across the main stereo buss. In other words, the entire mix is being compressed after any individual instruments (or groups of instruments) have been compressed and/or treated with any other effects. The purpose of buss compression is often described as helping to "glue" the mix together. Aside from helping to tame the levels a bit—i.e., bring down the peaks and boost the quiet points slightly—it helps give the mix a cohesion of sorts that helps all the various instruments and timbres balance more nicely together.

This is a subtle effect to be sure. Whereas compression can be used quite aggressively during the tracking and/or mixing stages to create certain desired effects, that's not generally the point of buss compression. Although it does create a noticeable effect, it's one of those effects that usually requires an A/B comparison to hear. However, it's an important step among the many in the mastering process that eventually add up to a sizeable difference in the end.

For buss compression duties, we'll make use of a standard stereo compressor. There are several different sorts of compressors, including **VCA** (Voltage Controlled Amplifier), **Opto** (which uses photocells and a light bulb), **Vari-Mu** (tube compressors), and **FET** (Field Effect Transistor) types. While these all compress the signal, they do so with different technologies (and, of course, the digital plugin versions of these all emulate the different technologies), resulting in very different sounds.

The most common of these types are generally agreed upon as follows:

- **VCA:** SSL (Solid State Logic)
- **Opto:** LA2A (originally manufactured by Teletronix, now by Universal Audio)
- **Vari-Mu:** Fairchild 670
- **FET:** 1176 (originally manufactured by UREI, now by Universal Audio)

The hardware versions of these compressors sell for thousands of dollars (in the case of a Fairchild 670, tens of thousands!), so most home recordists will have to settle for plugin emulations of them. Generally speaking, most people consider the VCA compressors most useful for buss compression duties. This is partly because they have extremely fast attack times and are therefore excellent at taming **transients** (the very beginning of a sound). They also tend to be very transparent while still adding a desirable "glue" to a mix. That said, emulations of an SSL-style buss compressor are very common, such as Waves' G-Master Buss Compressor, IK Multimedia's T-RackS Bus Compressor, or Native Instruments' Solid Bus Comp.

IK Multimedia T-RackS Bus Compressor

Waves SSL G-Master Buss Compressor

This isn't to say that the other compressor types are never used for buss compression. It's just that VCA compressors, such as the SSL-types, are the most common for the job. However, just as with clean or transparent EQs vs. colored ones, you should feel free to experiment with other types of compressors if you feel the mix is lacking character in some way. Some people prefer to use two (or more) different buss compressors in a row—perhaps a VCA followed by a Vari-Mu—to achieve the desired effect.

BUSS COMPRESSION TECHNIQUE

As with EQ, we're dealing with subtlety in buss compression as well. In other words, you're not going to be squashing things with 10 dB of gain reduction the way you may sometimes do while tracking or mixing. In this instance, we're going to be usually aiming for more of 1 to 2 dB of gain reduction—3 dB is considered quite aggressive at this point. We'll be starting with a fairly low ratio—maybe around 4:1 or lower—and adjusting the other controls (mainly attack and threshold) to achieve the gain reduction and sound we want.

As with compression on individual instruments in the mixing stage, you'll need to play with the attack and release times for each song until you get the desired effect. Many SSL-type compressors will default to a fast attack time (10 ms or less) and a very slow release time (over a second sometimes), but not all of them do, so be sure to check when you add your plugin. These defaults (fast attack/slow release) are usually a good place to start, so you can leave them as is and adjust the threshold until you're seeing around 2 dB of gain reduction during the loudest part of the song. This is very important, because if you make your settings during the verse, which is usually quieter than the chorus, then the compressor is probably going to be working much too hard in the chorus, creating unwanted effects.

*2 dB of gain reduction with
fast attack and slow release*

The slower the attack time, the more transients are going to get through. A slower attack time with a faster release can sometimes add excitement to a track, making those transients appear to "pop" a bit more. Keep in mind that, as you increase the attack time, you'll need to lower the threshold in order to achieve the same amount of gain reduction. This means the compressor will be working slightly harder and will have a greater effect on the overall sound.

*2 dB of gain reduction with
slow attack and fast release*

Make-Up Gain

A compressor's **make-up gain** is the boost in level that's added back to the signal after it's been compressed. Since compression, as an effect, essentially turns elements down, the signal needs to be boosted back up for the overall level to appear similar to what it was before it was compressed. This is a very important control in the mastering process, because failure to adjust it properly can result in fooling our ears with the "louder is better" phenomenon.

In other words, when comparing two sounds, we tend to perceive something louder as better or more desirable by habit. This means that if we have too much make-up gain on the compressor, we may think it sounds better just because it's louder than the bypassed signal. Conversely, if we have too little make-up gain on the compressor, then we may not think it's creating a positive effect simply because it's not as loud as the bypassed signal. Therefore, it's imperative that you adjust the compressor's make-up gain so that the active and bypassed levels are the same. This way, you can accurately determine what the compressor is doing to the track.

Master level with compressor bypassed

Compressed level lower than bypassed level

*Compressed level with makeup gain
added properly*

Compressor Transparency

Generally speaking, the harder the compressor is working, the more pronounced the differences will be from one model of compressor plugin to the next. So if you have more than one VCA-type compressor, then try comparing several of them with similar settings to hear the difference. (Just remember to bypass all but one of them at a time!) Some compressors will be much more transparent, while others will add their own sonic signature to the track.

If you're already happy with the sound and timbre of the un-mastered track, then you may want to use a transparent compressor so that you're only smoothing out levels and adding a bit of cohesion to the track. (The buss compressor found in Slate Digital's FG-X plugin is an example of one that's considered very transparent.) But if you feel the mix is lacking in excitement or clarity, then try a few different compressors to see if one can help in this regard. Each one will typically sound a bit different (or sometimes quite different)—even with the same settings—so it's worth the time to try them out. Considering how quickly this can be done today with plugins, you have no excuse!

LIMITING ▶

LIMITING TOOLBOX

At its most basic function, limiting is basically about protection. Especially in the digital age, **clipping** (the signal exceeding 0 dB) sounds very ugly and is to be avoided. That's where the **brickwall limiter** comes in. As its name implies, it allows you to set an unbreakable ceiling through which no signal can pass. This allows you to set the limit very close to 0 dB without worrying about signal breach.

As a general term, limiting is often described as compression with a high ratio—usually 10:1 or higher. Therefore, you can—assuming that you have the ratio settings available—achieve a limiting effect with a compressor. However, it's greatly recommended that you use a peak limiter (or brickwall limiter) instead, simply because they're specifically designed for the task. This means they'll usually feature controls that will be more intuitive and will often include other behind-the-scenes tricks that help them do the job in a more efficient manner.

There are plenty of options available in this department, including IZotope's Ozone Maximizer, Waves' L2 (or the newer L3-LL), IK Multimedia's T-RackS Stealth Limiter, Fabfilter's Pro-L 2, and Sonnox's Oxford Limiter V3. As with the different models of compressors, each one has its own sonic footprint, with some being more transparent than others.

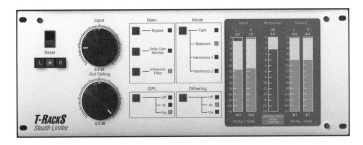

IK Multimedia T-RackS Stealth Limiter

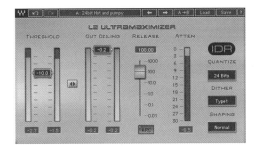

Waves L2 Ultramaximizer

The interface can greatly vary from model to model, so there may be a slight learning curve at first when trying out new models. Some may have more features than others, while some may be multi-band limiters (allowing you to limit the bass end differently than the mid-range or treble, for example) as opposed to single-band, etc. But they should all contain two main controls (though they may name them differently):

- **Ceiling (or margin):** This is the level above which no signal can pass. Most people set this at 0 dB or very close to it (such as -0.1, 0.3, -0.5, -1 dB etc.) to get the level as loud as possible without clipping.
- **Threshold (input or gain):** This control adjusts the amount of limiting that's occurring. Since most limiters have automatic make-up gain, increasing this control increases the loudness of the track.

As for the other features on your particular limiter, you may need to crack open the manual to get a complete understanding of what they do. Many limiters contain several different modes, which are each designed for different tasks. Some contain variable attack/release times, etc.

LIMITING TECHNIQUE

As with buss compression, you'll want to adjust your limiter while listening to the loudest section of the song to be sure you're hearing the full effect. And again, if you find yourself impacting the track so that you're getting 10 dB of gain reduction or other inadvertent effects, then you know you've gone too far. Depending on the track, a reduction of 3 to 5 dB is more common and still considered quite significant:

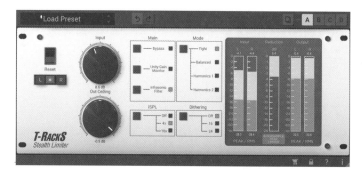

Output ceiling at -0.5 dB with 3.5 dB of gain reduction

As with compression, you can experiment with different attack and/or release times as well, assuming you have those controls on your limiter. The big issue to watch for when things get too slow, though, is **pumping**. This is the audible throbbing effect, usually caused by the bass, that's the result of too lenient attack and/or release times.

As some limiters do a better job at handling the peaks than others, regarding unwanted distortion and other artifacts, you'll have to use your ears and your own judgement when deciding how hard to push it. Just because the loudness wars have been in full effect for years now doesn't mean you have to fully participate in them! Never sacrifice sound quality for loudness alone.

Intersample Peaks (True Peaks)

The term **intersample peaks** refers to peaks that can occur between the digital samples. This is a phenomenon that can happen when the audio is converted from digital back into the analog in order to hear it through a speaker or headphones. These intersample peaks will normally go undetected by a limiter that's not equipped to handle them. Therefore, setting the limiter's ceiling at -1dB provides some extra headroom to help avoid any unwanted distortion when played through a less-than-stellar system.

Recently, more updated limiters feature **intersample peak detection** to deal with this. (Alternatively, you can use a **true peak meter** plugin after your limiter to basically achieve the same thing.) Although it's regularly touted on a plugin's stat sheet, the issue isn't quite as daunting as companies often make it seem. If you want to squeeze every single ounce of loudness out of a song that you can, then it may come in useful. But more often than not, you'll be able to achieve the effect you want without worry. Nevertheless, it does provide an additional safeguard, so if you do want that extra insurance, then you may want to make sure the next limiter you purchase has this feature or make use of a true peak meter to detect these intersample peaks.

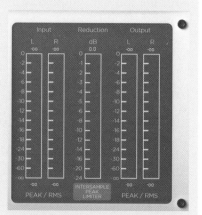

IK Multimedia's Stealth Limiter includes intersample peak detection

DITHERING ▶

Since we just talked about limiting, let's discuss the subject of **dither**, as it will typically be the next (and final) stage through which your audio passes. Dithering is a bit technical in the way it works, and we won't fully go into detail so as not to put everyone asleep, but we certainly can quickly discuss what it does and why we do it.

Basically, dither is random, quiet noise that's added to the signal to counter the effects of **quantization error**, which happens when we reduce the bit depth (or word length) of a digital audio signal. When working with audio in our DAW program, we're normally dealing with at least 32 or 64 bits, if not higher, these days. Even if we're working with a 24-bit file that we've imported into our DAW, the minute we make any alteration to it—adjust the volume, add a plugin, etc.—we're dealing with a higher bit count behind the scenes. This means that, even if we're then mixing down to a 24-bit file, we'll still be reducing the bit count.

Obviously, we normally think of adding any noise as undesirable, but it's important to note here that we're talking about very low-level noise that's usually inaudible because it's completely masked by the music. So dithering is certainly the lesser of two evils in this regard, because the other options—**truncation** (simply lopping off the leftover bits after file size reduction) and **rounding off** (rounding each bit to the nearest whole number after file size reduction)—produce fewer desirable results.

So the short and simple explanation is that you always need to dither whenever you produce your final master.

WHEN AND HOW TO DITHER

So how do we dither, and when do we apply it? In regard to the "when," that's easy—it's always the last thing that happens to the audio. Typically, this will directly occur after the limiting, which will be the final plugin in your typical mastering chain. You don't want anything else done to the audio after dither is applied.

The "how" is not quite as straightforward simply because there are various ways to apply it. Mainly, you have the choice to apply it with a plugin or during the rendering process in your DAW.

Applying Dither with a Plugin

Many mastering suites or limiting plugins feature a dither module within them, enabling you to add dither at that point. Some plugins will feature more options than others, including various types and amounts of dither, noise-shaping, etc. You can experiment with these settings if you want to get academic about it. In most situations, though, you'd be hard pressed to hear a significant difference, because dithering is generally inaudible.

More important is the **bit resolution setting**. If the plugin features dither, then it will almost certainly allow you to choose between at least 16 and 24 bits, among others. This is the critical step—make sure you choose the appropriate bit size for your target medium of choice (16 bits for a CD, etc.).

Izotope Ozone plugin with several options for dithering

IK Multimedia T-RackS Stealth Limiter plugin with basic dithering options only

If dithering is a part of a limiting or mastering plugin, then it will appear at the end of the chain by default. (Definitely leave it there!) If your mastering suite doesn't have a dithering module, then you can use a dedicated dithering plugin instead. Some DAWs come with one, but if yours doesn't, then you can find many third-party plugins. Just remember to place it last in the effects chain on your master buss.

Applying Dither During the Rendering Process

If you don't have access to a dithering plugin, then many DAWs have a dithering feature that can be applied during the rendering process. The important thing to remember here is that you don't want to double-dither! In other words:

- If you're dithering with a plugin, then make sure the dithering feature is turned off when you render.
- If you're not dithering with a plugin, then make sure the dithering feature is turned on when you render.

*Reaper rendering screen with
dithering options*

CHAPTER 3
FIXING THE MIX

In this chapter, we're going to deal with the issue of troublesome mixes. This is something that will usually only come up if you're mastering someone else's music or perhaps an older recording of your own, for which you no longer have the individuals tracks for re-mixing. Otherwise, these types of issues would be better addressed with a entirely new mix. However, there will most likely be times that arise when you come across a track that could have been mixed better, and the only thing you have to work to work with is a stereo file. When that's the case, doing your best with the tools available is the only option (save for re-recording the whole song, which we'll assume is not an option).

So let's take a look at a few mixes that suffer from some common issues and discuss ways in which we can lend them a helping hand in the mastering process. Of course, every song is different, so you may not run into these issues exactly. However, working through them should give you some ideas on how to attack other specific issues that you may face in the future.

THE HARSH MIX ▶

This is a common issue. Often in search of clarity and excitement, many amateur mixers end up producing a mix that sounds a bit harsh and unpleasant for one or more reasons. This can be related to one specific instrument that's sticking out too much, or it can be a more general buildup of unpleasant frequencies. Some of the most common culprits for harshness are ride cymbals, guitars, and vocals.

REACH FOR THE EQ?
The first thought that may come to mind is the use of EQ. You can boost a parametric band and sweep up and down until you've located the offending frequency. Once you've zeroed in on it, then apply the necessary cut.

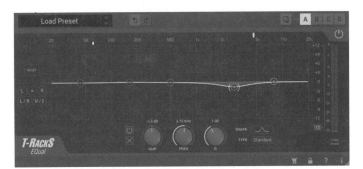

Sweeping with large boost to find offending frequency

Applying moderate cut at 2.75 kHz

While this can be an effective tool at removing a harsh frequency, it usually comes at a cost when you're dealing with only a stereo track. This is because you'll also be affecting everything else in that frequency region as well. What this means is that, while you may be taming the harshness of an overly bright ride cymbal, for instance, you could also be stripping the track of some upper-mid excitement or presence in the snare, guitars, vocals, etc.

This is because EQ—as powerful a tool as it can be—is a **static** process. In other words, once it's on, it stays on and does not change (without automation, of course). You could try to get very specific with your frequency and Q setting, thereby doing as little damage as possible to the surrounding instruments. But the offending instrument or region is often times a bit too broad for this to be practical. No matter how hard you try, you'll most likely end up affecting other areas more than you want to.

AN ALTERNATIVE SOLUTION: MULTI-BAND COMPRESSION
Perhaps a better solution is the use of a **multi-band compressor** (or **dynamic EQ**). Compression is a **non-static** process because compressors constantly change their behavior based on what's being fed into them. This means that, with proper settings, you'll be doing less peripheral damage than when using an EQ alone. A multi-band compressor allows you to compress specific frequency ranges instead of the entire spectrum. So, for example, you could have little or no compression on the bass end while heavily compressing the top end if you wanted. Alternatively, you could compress only the mid-range, leaving the bass and treble ranges completely alone.

Multi-Band Compressor Toolbox

Most multi-band compressors have from three to five customizable frequency ranges. You can usually set the boundaries of these ranges yourself, which affords very exacting means of control. A common default setting would be bass, low-mid, high-mid, and treble ranges, for example. Beyond that, each band can usually be engaged or bypassed individually, allowing you to leave certain regions of the frequency range completely untouched if you want.

IK Multimedia T-RackS Quad Comp

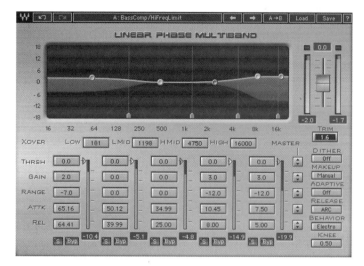

Waves Linear Phase Multiband Compressor

Beyond that, each frequency band will usually feature a full set of controls commonly found on a normal compressor, which can include threshold, attack/release, ratio, etc. This means you can apply completely different compressions to each band. Another handy feature is that you can usually solo a frequency band and listen only to that range to identify the specific troublesome frequency.

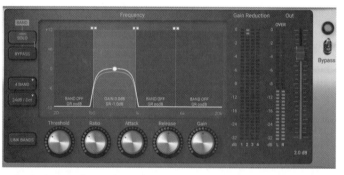

Soloing a band with a multi-band compressor

If you have only one problem area that needs to be tamed, then one alternative to a multi-brand compressor is a compressor with a selectable frequency range, such as the Oxford SuprEsser by Sonnox. These are sometimes called dynamic EQs or **de-essers** as well. This is technically a single-band compressor, but you can select the specific frequency range you want to compress. It also allows you to listen in three modes: the whole mix, outside mode (only the frequencies outside your compression range), and inside mode (only the frequencies inside your compression range). These modes are another great way of zeroing in on the problem frequencies.

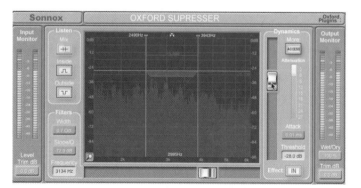

Sonnox Oxford SuprEsser

In short, the multi-band compressor (or dynamic EQ) is a powerful tool for the mastering process. Though it's not uncommon to make use of all the bands, it's also useful when you need to concentrate on only one specific frequency.

Multi-Band Compressor Technique

In our example dealing with a harsh mix, we can make use of the multi-band compressor's ability to only affect a specific range. Using either an EQ or the band-soloing feature of the multi-band compressor to isolate the harsh frequencies, we can then apply the desired amount of compression to that range, taming the harshness while doing far less damage to the rest of the material.

For instance, if we have an obnoxiously loud ride cymbal, then we can identify its range and compress it alone while leaving the bass and treble untouched:

Multi-band compressor with mid band centered
on 2.75k, applying compression

You can also experiment with the make-up gain, adding some of it back to retrieve any lost excitement if necessary. Though this may seem somewhat counterintuitive, it's not undoing the work the compressor has already done. It's still pushing down the offending frequency and taming it, so when the make-up gain is added back in, the frequency will be sticking out much less:

Multi-band compressor with mid band centered
on 2.75k and make-up gain added

By experimenting with the range of the active band and the various compression settings, you should be able to make a significant dent in the problem area without overly affecting the rest of the track in a negative way.

THE THUMPY MIX ▶

Another very common mark of an amateur mix is the thumpy or boomy mix. This is usually the result of someone mixing in an untreated room or one that's not well-suited for critical listening. It could also be due to mixing on headphones that aren't producing enough bass frequencies. Whatever the case, the bass frequencies are not being accurately represented on the mixer's system, and he or she is compensating by turning up or down the bass more than it should be. In the case of the boomy mix, the bass is being turned up too much.

Oftentimes, there will be one instrument—such as the kick drum or bass guitar—that's the main culprit in this scenario. When this happens, again, it's tough to undo the damage when working from only a stereo track because you'll again be affecting everything in that range. This is why the multi-band compressor is usually a better tool than an EQ; it only affects things when it's triggered, thereby leaving more of the track untouched.

For example, if you have a kick drum that's too loud, then you don't want to punish the entire bottom end—you just want to affect the kick. And since the kick is not a static instrument—i.e., it's not a sine wave, etc.—it makes more sense to use a dynamic processor that will only engage when needed. By contrast, an EQ will always be making its mark on the track, which means it will also be cutting out other important low-end frequencies such as the bass guitar, guitars, male vocals, etc. This usually results in a damaged, thinned-out bottom end.

So the first thing we need to do is determine the range of the bottom band on the multi-band compressor. For this, we can solo the band and listen to it to determine how far down the problem extends:

Soloing bottom band of multi-band compressor

Once we've identified the problem area, then we can start to apply the necessary compression to tame the issue. If you're dealing with a percussive instrument like a kick drum, then you'll need to pay close attention to the attack and release times to make sure you're not getting any pumping or other unwanted artifacts. Generally speaking, you may be looking for about 3–5 dB of gain reduction in this case with a fairly quick attack of roughly 10 ms and a release at around 100–130 ms:

Compressing low end with 3 dB gain reduction

Again, experimentation is key, especially when dealing with something as momentary as a kick drum. The attack and release times can make a big difference in how the compression affects the audio.

THE LOUD HI-HAT

The hi-hat is another very common trouble-maker in mixes, as it's often too loud or too bright (if not both). Since this is another instrument-specific problem, a compromise is needed to fix the issue. This is because we're no doubt going to affecting some other instruments in that area, including the top end of the vocals, guitars, and more. But again, mastering is a game of the big picture, so in this case, we have to go with the lesser of two evils.

The first step is to determine the offending frequency range of the hi-hat. Unfortunately, the hi-hat can cover a deceptively large frequency range, often extending from the upper-mids to well within the treble range. A good ballpark range may be from about 3–12 kHz, but you'll need to experiment a bit more to really zero in on it. In order to do this, it's helpful to make use of both the "outside the band" and "inside the band" listening tricks, as you can on the Oxford SuprEsser. In other words, first establish the frequency range of your active band on the compressor, and then listen to everything outside of that range. You can then move or expand/contract the range to see if you can get the hi-hat to mostly disappear. Once you've done that, listen to what's inside the range to see if it mostly contains hi-hat.

If necessary, go back and forth a few times with these two methods to zero in on it the best you can.

If you can't listen "outside the band," then you can still zero in fairly well by listening inside the band—otherwise known as "soloing the band." Most multi-band compressors, dynamic EQs, or de-essers should have this ability. Just be sure to solo the frequency band before you've applied any compression so you can hear the purest representation of that band.

*Soloing a band in IK Multimedia's T-RackS
Quad Comp*

Once you've set your range, then it's time to apply compression. In the case of the hi-hat, you'll want a very fast attack time (well under 1 ms if you can) and a quick release time as well (around 100 ms or so). Depending on the severity of the issue, you'll need to adjust the threshold and ratio to get the necessary gain reduction. This is where the trade-off happens. When compressing the hi-hat, you'll be affecting a few other things as well, but hopefully, we won't be doing too much damage.

Remember to frequently bypass and compare the affected and unaffected signal to make sure you're on the right track. You can also adjust the make-up gain to see if you can restore some of the life you may have removed with the compression without bringing back too much of the offending hi-hat:

Applying compression to tame the hi-hat

GETTING BACK A BIT OF WHAT YOU'VE LOST

If you're satisfied with how you've tamed the hi-hat but feel that you've shaved off too much high end in the process, then you can salvage some of this by adding an EQ after the multi-band compressor. Use a standard band or add a high shelf to see which works better. This will undoubtably bring back some of the hi-hat, but the hope is that it won't be as obnoxious as before.

You may want to go back and forth between the multi-band and the EQ, increasing the compression (and therefore removing more of the hi-hat) with the knowledge that you're going to be adding the EQ back to recover some of the highs in the rest of the track. You can experiment adjusting both the multi-band and the EQ in an interactive manner until you reach the desired compromise.

*Restoring some top end with a high shelf EQ
after the multi-band compressor*

It should be mentioned that this EQ recovery technique can also be used with other instruments or ranges, including our earlier kick drum or ride cymbal examples. Again, experiment with shelving vs. bell (adjustable frequency and Q) techniques to see which yields the best results.

CHAPTER 4
MID/SIDE PROCESSING AND PHASE

Another aspect of the mastering process deals with what's known as **mid/side (M/S) processing**. As the name implies, this involves working with material that's mostly contained either within the middle or along the sides of the stereo spectrum. There are a few different reasons why this is necessary, and that's one of the subjects of this chapter. We'll also spend some time talking about the issue of **phase** and why it's important.

MID/SIDE PROCESSING ▶

Simply put, M/S processing deals with affecting the sides of a mix rather than the entire spectrum. This means that anything that's panned more or less up the middle—usually vocals, snare drum, kick drum, bass, etc.—remains completely untouched. This makes M/S processing quite a powerful tool. For example, we don't want to compromise the integrity of the lead vocal just because we need to address an issue with the guitar that's panned to the side.

As we'll see, there are many applications for M/S processing, and this is one reason why so many mastering plugins (EQs, compressors, etc.) have built-in M/S capabilities. Of course, it should be mentioned that just because you have the capability to do this doesn't mean you should. If a mix doesn't need any help in this regard, then you shouldn't feel the need to force the issue just because you want to play with all your toys! However, chances are you will find some benefit from this powerful tool in most mixes you encounter.

MID/SIDE PROCESSING TOOLBOX
There are numerous plugins with M/S capabilities, and they can all be useful depending on your specific needs. Some are solely dedicated to M/S processing and have a limited number of features, such as Waves' Center, while others add additional stereo-widening and other features, such as IK Multimedia's T-RackS Quad Image or Waves' S1 Stereo Imager. There are many other plugins—such as EQs, multi-band compressors, etc.—that also have M/S capabilities as well. These are almost always included with any mastering suite software, such as iZotope's Ozone or Steinberg's Wavelab Pro.

IK Multimedia T-RackS Quad Image

Waves Center

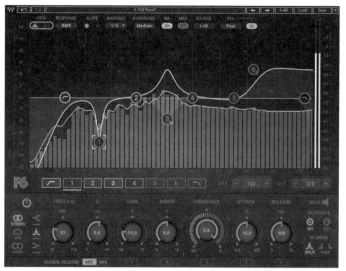

Waves F6 Floating-Band Dynamic EQ

The most important feature for our purposes is the ability to control the levels of the mid and sides independently, which all of the above-mentioned plugins will do. Secondary features, such as adjusting the stereo width, depth, and panning are helpful as well, as we'll see later during this chapter.

M/S TECHNIQUE 1: FIXING AN IMBALANCED MIX OR STEM

Firstly, we'll look at a common issue of amateur mixers: a lopsided or imbalanced mix (or stem). This imbalance could be due to an instrument (such as a guitar) that's too loud and/or panned too wide relative to the rest of the track. It could also simply be an imbalance in the overall mix, in which too many things are panned to one side, creating a lopsided feel. Whatever the case, we can tackle the issue with M/S processing.

Now, if you're asking, "Why can't I fix the issue by panning?" then that's an understandable question. Some of these issues can be adequately solved by simply adjusting the panning. But M/S processing gives us much more control than a pan knob, allowing us to tackle more demanding issues than panning can handle. Plus, it's simply more convenient to make all the adjustments in one place.

So let's say we have a mix that sounds left-heavy. If we simply grab the pan knob and turn it to the right, then we may balance the levels out, but we'll also be moving some important center elements of the mix to the right in the process, which we probably don't want to do. However, by using M/S processing, we're able to select only the sides and pan those to the right, thereby leaving the center elements alone.

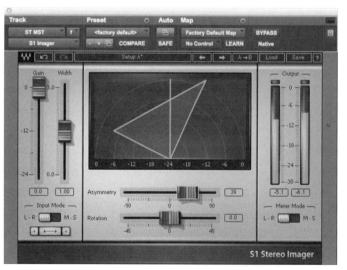

Panning the sides to the right with the Waves S1

If you find that, once you've corrected the balance, the sides lack some of the power they had before, then there are other options available. Many of the more full-featured plugs, such as the Brainworx bx_XL V2, offer the additional capability of limiting the sides or mids independently, thereby allowing you to recover some of the gain that may have been lost while balancing out the sides.

Recovering some lost gain in the side channels with the Brainworx bx_XL V2 after balancing the left-heavy track

M/S TECHNIQUE 2: WIDENING ▶

Another common use for M/S processing is **widening**. This can be applied to a mix that sounds very narrow, in which we're trying our best to spread things out a bit and create some perceived room. Alternatively, it can be used with more subtlety, creating the illusion of slightly more width on tracks that don't sound all that narrow to begin with.

The Narrow Mix

If you're dealing with a mix that's simply too narrow, then a widening plugin can make a significant difference. (Again, the ideal solution is to remix the song with the appropriate panning, etc., but we're assuming here that you only have a stereo track or stem at your disposal.) It's not a magical fix by any means, but it can significantly help declutter the middle, which is crucial if you're dealing with a pop song, in which the vocals usually need to be the center of attention.

Widening a Mono Mix?

It's important to note that the tips here are meant to be used with stereo mixes. The mixes may be narrow, but the important part is that they are stereo. If you have a mono mix and want to widen it, then that's a different story. Using M/S processing alone isn't going to magically create a stereo image from a mono mix. The best you can do is create a "false stereo" sound with a few different methods, but it's not going to be true stereo. Applying standard widening to a mono mix is simply going to make the track louder because the "mid" and "sides" contain the same material.

Depending on how narrow the mix is, you need to be careful with how wide you go, as it can eventually start to sound somewhat unnatural. We certainly don't want to do more harm than good, but we can still apply a good bit of widening to help make more room in the middle.

For this basic type of widening, something as simple as a Waves S1 could be all you need. With this type of plugin, there's generally a control labeled "Width" or "Spread," and you simply raise it up to increase the widening effect.

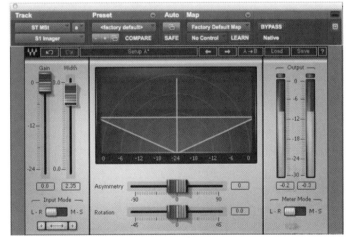

Increasing the perceived width with the Waves S1 plugin

Keep an ear out for some unwanted artifacts with this process, though. For example, you may find that the bass guitar gets pushed out to one side, which is normally not desirable. If you do experience this phenomenon, then you may need to try another widening approach by chiefly using a widener that has some frequency-specific capabilities. For example, IK Multimedia's Quad Image allows you to select up to four adjustable frequency bands, affecting the width of each band independently. This means you can leave the low frequencies alone and spread out only the mid and/or high frequencies.

Using IK Multimedia's Quad Image plugin to spread out the hi-mids and highs only

Solidifying the Sides

Sometimes a mix may not be narrow, but the sides may sound slightly too disparate or fluid. This is largely a matter of subjectivity, of course, but if you want a more cohesive sound altogether, then use M/S compression to create the illusion of widening, thereby tightening up the sound.

For this task, we can use a multi-band compressor with M/S capabilities, such as Waves' F6 Floating-Band Dynamic EQ, Izotope Ozone, or something similar. You'll want to make sure you're in M/S mode (most of these types of processors allow you to select from a few different modes, such as L/R, M/S, etc.), and you'll want to select only the sides for processing. You can then apply compression to only the sides, solidifying them in the process.

A ratio of around 4:1 is usually a good place to start with this type of process. Adjust the threshold until you achieve the desired effect, and then add make-up gain to restore the volume. Though we've not actually used any widening processing, this will often create the illusion of a slightly wider mix while leaving the center completely untouched.

Solidifying the sides with M/S compression

Another way to create a similar effect is to do the same thing with EQ. In other words, we can use an EQ with M/S capabilities, such as the one found in Izotope's Ozone, to excite the sides a bit and create the illusion of widening. The process is similar to that of the M/S compression. First, make sure you've selected the side mode for processing. Then, sweep around to find a pleasant frequency that you'd like to enhance on the sides.

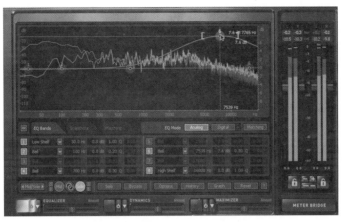

Exciting the sides with EQ

Conversely, if you feel the sides are already too excited and are distracting from the vocal and other important center elements (snare, etc.), then you can slightly dull them down the same way by simply cutting instead of boosting. To avoid losing any power, you could combine this approach with some M/S compression as well.

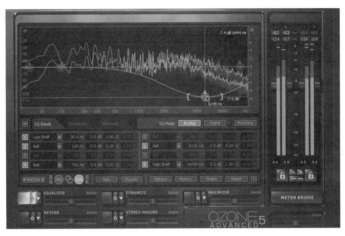

Dulling down the sides with EQ

PHASE ▶

Let's quickly discuss the subject of phase and how it can become problematic in certain cases. Although phase issues are more common when dealing with pairs of channels— for example, overhead drum mics or amped and D.I. bass tracks—there can be instances when one instrument (or stem) is out of phase with the rest of the mix.

IDENTIFYING PHASE ISSUES

Although phasing problems can be at times obvious when listening, at other times it's more difficult to pick out. To this end, it can be helpful to make use of a **sound field phase meter**, such as the classic PAZ Position by Waves or Insight by Izotope. These plugins will give you a physical representation of phasing issues, thereby allowing you to identify where any problems may lie. For example, in Waves' PAZ Position, anything that's anti-phase shows up as horizontal spikes as opposed to the more vertical spikes for the in-phase audio.

*With the Waves PAZ Position plug, anything that's out of phase shows up
in the bottom portion of the display, outside the "in-phase" portion.*

MONO COMPATIBILITY

If you find that, when a given instrument enters, you begin seeing a great deal of anti-phase activity, then you can most likely identify that instrument as a phase issue. While the problem may not seem terribly obvious to everyone in the normal stereo mix—some people are more affected by and/or sensitive to out-of-phase sounds than others—it can become quite problematic regarding mono compatibility.

If a given instrument is largely out of phase compared to the rest of the mix, it can almost entirely disappear when the mix is heard in mono. Granted, the idea of hearing our mixes in mono isn't something we usually think about these days, but it's still not uncommon at all for some music to be streamed in mono on the internet for the purpose of saving data, etc. There are also some smartphones, clock radios, etc., that play in mono as well, so it is something that still should be considered. (Granted, all smartphones should have a stereo headphone jack, but sometimes they only have a built-in mono speaker.)

The bad news is that there's really nothing you can do to remedy this type of issue at the mastering stage. This is another good reason that you should always check your mixes in mono before submitting them to a mastering engineer!

CHAPTER 5
MORE MIX FIXES

In this chapter, we'll look at a few more fixes for some specific issues we haven't dealt with thus far. These include considerations for vinyl mastering and flat or dull mixes that lack punch and excitement. By this point in the book, you'll most likely have some ideas on how to tackle these issues, as the tools we'll use will be many of the same we've used before.

VINYL CONSIDERATIONS ▶

Firstly, let's talk about a few things to consider when your final product is going to be transferred to vinyl. Whether or not anyone foresaw it, vinyl has made quite the resurgence as of late. It's hard to believe, but vinyl records were projected to outsell CDs in 2019 for the first time since 1986, continuing this trend in 2020. In fact, both CDs and vinyl records have toppled digital download sales for the first time in years as well. Granted, both versions of physical media still pale in comparison to the new king of the hill—streaming subscription-based services—which account for over 60% of all music revenue in the U.S. Nevertheless, it's clear that vinyl is worthy of consideration once again, so it's a good idea to spend a bit of time talking about some issues that can arise when mastering for it.

SIBILANCE

This is a big one because it's often very problematic for vinyl. The short story is that excessive **sibilance** (consonant sounds in speech or singing) and aggressive high end leads to distortion on vinyl. The reason for this has to do with how the vinyl is produced. For technical reasons, during the cutting process, the bass is attenuated while the treble is boosted. Conversely, when played back on a turntable, an inverse EQ curve is applied (boosted bass and attenuated highs), resulting in a flat response.

The result of this process is a longer running time—i.e., more music can fit on a disc—but it comes at a price, which is the inability to handle excessive high end. If the highs are boosted too much on the master, then overly complex grooves occur during the cutting process, which are many times too difficult for turntable needles to correctly trace, resulting in distorted playback.

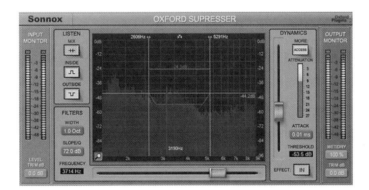

*De-essers, such as Sonnox's Oxford SuprEsser,
are often the tool of choice for taming
harsh sibilance.*

LOUDNESS WARS: JUST SAY NO!

Simply put, excessive volume can create issues for vinyl. This basically means that all the brick-wall limiting you apply to achieve an acceptable amount of clipping for CD or digital audio will result in more distortion when heard on vinyl. The solution is a simple one—slightly back off the signal level and don't aim for a completely maxed out waveform. You don't want to go too low, of course, because then you'll start to worry about dealing with the **S/N (signal to noise) ratio** of the vinyl format. But shaving off a bit of signal level as compared to a digital master is probably a safe bet.

TAKE CARE WITH THE BASS FREQUENCIES

Another issue that can cause problems for vinyl concerns the bass frequencies. Simply put, bass frequencies need to be mono. So, for example, if you've got a chorused bass guitar that's spread out or a wide stereo bass synth, then those could spell trouble for a vinyl record. Again, the reasoning has to do with the cutting process and how the grooves are formed. Phasing issues in the low frequencies can cause grooves to collapse, which results in skips on playback. A good rule of thumb is to simply keep frequencies below about 120 Hz in mono.

Fortunately, we can compensate for this even if we only have the stereo mix at our disposal. The tool of choice is mid/side processing. What you need is simply an EQ with M/S capabilities, such as Izotope's Ozone or IK Multimedia's EQual. Engage the M/S mode and select only the sides for processing. Then, apply a high-pass filter at about 120 Hz, slightly adjusting up or down until the proper result is achieved. Compare the processed signal with the bypassed one to ensure you've sufficiently narrowed the bass frequencies, and you're good to go!

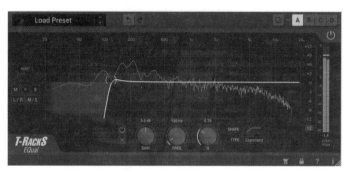

Applying a high-pass filter to only the side channel with IK Multimedia's EQual plugin

TRACK SEQUENCING AND RUNNING TIME

It's helpful to keep the track sequence in mind when mastering for vinyl because of the significant difference it makes. For technical reasons, the frequency response on vinyl is different by the time the needle reaches the inside of the record. Specifically, the response around 15 kHz is reduced by about 3 dB. What this means is that you generally want to avoid placing the loudest songs as the last song on a side. It's better to place softer ballads there.

Also, the maximum suggested running time per side should be noted as well. Simply put, the louder the music, the more space it takes up on a record. This basically means the louder your master track, the less playing time per side you'll have on vinyl. Therefore, you may want to adjust fades ins/outs if it means you can confine within certain running times. You should consult with the pressing plant for more details on the requirements and suggestions on this topic.

PROBLEM MIX #1—FLAT AND LIFELESS ▶️

Now, let's turn our attention to something that's a bit more subtle. In some cases, a mix isn't necessarily too boomy, shrill, or honky, etc., but it just lacks a bit of excitement or punch. Of course, we can't work miracles in the mastering process, but what we can usually do—aside from raising the level, etc.—is add "icing" on top to give it that final sheen that's sometimes missing.

TRANSIENT SHAPER

One possible fix for a flat mix is the use of a **transient shaper** (also called a **transient modulator** or **transient designer**). This is a versatile plugin that's designed to enhance or diminish transients. Common transient sounds include the pick on a guitar string, the stick hitting the drumhead, etc. They're often used on drums, guitars, reverb trails, and many other instruments, especially during the mixing process. But they can sometimes help bring a lifeless-sounding mix to life, as well.

Whereas a compressor works with the whole signal, and therefore will change the level of the track, the transient shaper works only with the initial transient of the sound, leaving the overall level of the track intact. It also produces a different effect due to the fact that it's only working on the first part of a signal.

TRANSIENT SHAPER TOOLBOX

Transient shapers come as dedicated plugins and as additional features on some mastering suites. Most of them will have at least three basic controls—often labeled attack, sustain, and gain—but many models feature additional controls for enhanced precision. Popular plugins include Sonnox's Oxford Transmod and SPL's Transient Designer, the latter of which is more often used on individual instruments like drums, guitar, etc.

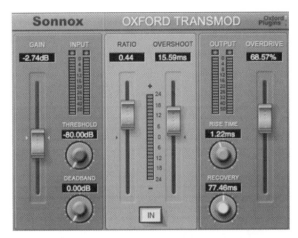

*Sonnox's Oxford Transmod is a basic, single-band transient design-
er with several additional features for more precise shaping.*

Some transient shapers allow you to only work with specific frequency bands. In other words, they act like a multi-band compressor, only with transients. This additional control allows for very precise sound tailoring, as you can focus on bringing out the transient of the kick drum, for instance, if the rest of the mix doesn't need the same attention. The Waves Trans-X Multi and Izotope Neuron 2 are popular choices for multi-band transient shapers.

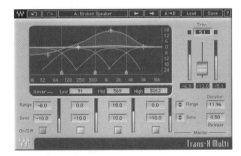

Waves' Trans-X Multi plugin allows for multi-band transient shaping.

TRANSIENT SHAPER TECHNIQUES

When using a transient shaper to enhance or boost the transients (they can usually be used to deemphasize the transients as well if the mix is too snappy), it's helpful to start out on relatively level ground. This is because if certain instruments—like the snare for example—are already sticking out a bit in the mix, then boosting with a transient shaper will tend to make those instruments stick out even more, creating a more imbalanced mix. Therefore, we can place a buss compressor before the transient shaper to help even things out before we start trying to bring out those attacks.

As is usually the case with buss compression, we're not going to be crushing things here. A gain reduction around 1 or 2 dB should most likely do the trick.

*Gluing together the elements of the mix with IK
Multimedia's Bus Compressor before applying
the transient shaper*

Once you've applied some buss compression, then you're ready for the transient shaper. Many of them have controls similar to a compressor, including a threshold, ratio, attack/release, and gain, and therefore the operation should feel fairly intuitive. However, regarding the gain, it's important to remember that, assuming you're boosting the transients (as would be the case on a flat-sounding mix), you'll most likely be increasing the level, as opposed to decreasing it, which is the case with compressors. Therefore, you may need to lower the gain after processing the transients rather than bringing it up.

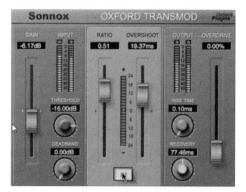

*Notice the gain has been lowered here to
compensate for the increased level after processing.*

If you need to add excitement or punch to only one frequency range— for instance, if the bass sounds flat or the treble is lacking excitement—then try a multi-band transient designer, such as the Waves Trans-X Multi or Izotope's Neuron 2. Firstly, you need to determine which area needs processing, and then you can adjust the crossover(s) to single out the frequency band you want.

For example, if you want to add more punch to the kick and/or bass guitar, then work with the lowest band and set the crossover at around 120 Hz. Then, you can adjust the threshold and ratio or sensitivity, along with the various time parameters—duration and/or release times—to achieve the desired punch.

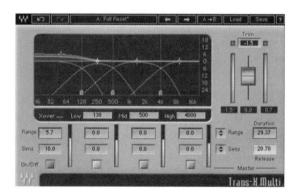

*Adding punch to the bass frequencies with the
Waves Trans-X Multi plugin.*

Conversely, if you have an area that has too much attack, then you can zone in on it and deemphasize the transients to help mellow it out. For instance, if the pick sounds on an acoustic guitar are too prominent, then you might work with the upper-mid band, adjusting the crossovers to best isolate the area and turning down the transients for a smoother overall sound.

PROBLEM MIX #2—IMBALANCED, DRY, AND LACKING DEPTH ▶

Now, let's deal with another mix scenario that has a few more issues than the previous one. In this scenario, we'll assume we have a mix with a sizzling, excessive top end—as can often be the case with a drum machine hi-hat, for example—that sticks out like a sore thumb. The mix will also be dry and lacking in depth. This is common when electronic sounds—drum machines, synthesizers, etc.—are used with factory-made sounds and aren't tailored at all with any additional processing. On top of that, we'll imagine that there's a thumping 808-style kick sound that's excessively loud.

In a mix with multiple issues such as this, we're going to make use of many small steps to achieve the effect we want. Trying to correct all the issues with one or two wide-sweeping processes isn't going to cut it here. Instead, we need to perform several more surgical moves in tandem, which will add up to a larger effect in the end.

First off, we'll start with a multi-band compressor to help tame the top and bottom end. Since we only want to affect the bass and treble regions at this point, we need at least a three-band compressor because we want to establish a middle ground that's not affected at all. It's helpful to solo the bands when setting the crossover points so you can really zero in on the sounds that are going to be affected. Once you have the crossovers properly set, then experiment with the settings for each band to achieve the desired result. For a boomy electronic kick sound, we'll need a fairly short attack with a release time that's on the slightly longer side. Assuming the high-end sizzle is coming from a hi-hat, we'll need a quick attack time there as well, though probably not quite as long of a release.

*Compressing the low and high ends with
IK Multimedia's Quad Comp*

After taming the extremities, we'd like to inject a bit of "vibe" into the track to provide some much-needed depth and complexity. For this, we're going to first turn to an analog console emulation plugin, such as the Waves NLS Summer or Slate Digital's Virtual Preamp Collection. Many of these types of plugins emulate classic consoles by the likes of Neve, API, and SSL, among others, and they can often help add an extra dimension to a mix.

Often times, there aren't a great deal of parameters to adjust on this type of plugin. You'll usually have some type of input gain, trim, or drive parameter. It's just a matter of adjusting that parameter until you hear the sound you're looking for.

*Adding depth and character with the Waves NLS
plugin set to emulate a Neve console*

Next, let's use a virtual tape emulation plugin to help slightly smooth out and/or decrease the top end while providing some more saturation and color. Several companies make tape emulators, including Slate Digital's Virtual Tape Machine, Waves' Abbey Road Studios J37, Avid's Reel Tape Saturation, and IK Multimedia's T-RackS Tape Machines Collection. Most of these emulators offer several parameters, including tape speed, tape type, input/output gain, bias adjustment, etc., allowing you to get specific with the desired effect. You should certainly experiment with all these variables, as they will all be slightly different.

Adding additional warm and saturation with
IK Multimedia's T-RackS Tape Machine 80

After stacking two colorizing and saturating plugins atop one another—i.e., the console and tape machine emulators—listen to see if any frequencies are building up, especially in the lower end. In our example, let's say that we're starting to get a bit thick around the 260 Hz area. This instance might be a nice spot to tame with a simple parametric EQ.

Taming the low-frequency build up around 260 Hz with
Universal Audio's Massenburg Designworks MDWEQ5

If the track is truly and uncomfortably dry, then consider adding reverb to help open things up. Granted, this is an extreme case, and adding reverb during the mastering stage is a rare thing indeed. But we'll look at this just to show the range of what we're talking about here. We'll use a room reverb for this with a very short decay of less than 400 ms, and we'll blend in very little compared to the dry mix. This is a very subtle effect for sure, but again, all these subtle touches work together to create something substantial in the end.

Adding a touch of reverb with IK Multimedia's T-RackS
Classik Room reverb

Finally, before we use the limiter, let's add a bit of top-end sheen. Of course, this may seem a bit counterintuitive, as we've been going to great lengths in order to get rid of the sizzling high end all along. However, the idea is that, hopefully, the track—including the top end—will sound more balanced overall, which means that when we do add this sheen on top, it won't be accentuating the nasty sizzle that was there at the beginning. Kush Audio's Clariphonic—or the more recent mkII version—is an excellent choice in this regard. It doesn't feature many controls, but it works very well at what it does.

Adding a top-end sheen with Kush Audio's Clariphonic

Now, we'll wrap things up with the limiter to raise the volume. We may even choose to use a buss compressor before applying the limiter, just to glue things together a bit more. Considering all the work we've done with the track, the buss compressor will have a much easier time bringing the elements together at this point in the chain. Depending on how transparent your compressor is, you don't want too much reduction at this point. If it's a transparent-sounding compressor, such as Slate Digital's FG Comp, then you could probably hit 1.5 or 2 dB of reduction and do just fine.

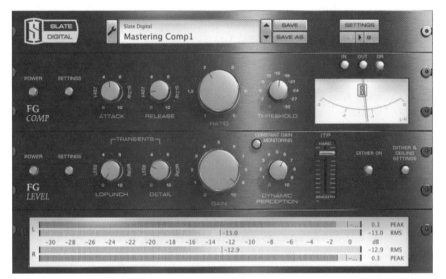

Using Slate Digital's FG-X for buss compression and limiting

As you can see, we made use of a good number of plugins altogether, but they each had a specific purpose. Each one sort of plowed the road for the next, and they all worked together to create the final result. In particularly troublesome tracks, this type of approach will usually be required, since the numerous problems will each likely require more specific attention.

CHAPTER 6
STEMS AND MASTERING

Until this point in the book, we've been primarily talking about what we can do with a stereo mix. At a few points, we've mentioned how it would be nice to have access to the individual tracks because there are some fixes that simply aren't possible given only a stereo track. But now we'll deal with something slightly different: the world of mastering with stems.

MASTERING WITH STEMS ▶

WHAT ARE STEMS?

Firstly, let's define the term **stem**, as some people still seem a bit confused by the word. A stem is a stereo track that usually contains common elements of an audio production mixed together. In other words, it's a **submix**. For example, you may have a guitar stem, which would typically include all the guitar parts of the song. This would be a stereo file in which all the guitars would be panned, EQ'd, processed with effects, etc. the same way they were in the DAW session. Then, you may have a drum stem, which would be a stereo track containing all the processed drum sounds, etc.

Even though some people use the terms interchangeably, stems are not the same as **multi tracks**. The multi tracks of a project are simply each individual track—usually mono tracks but sometimes stereo—all collected in a folder and ready to be imported to another DAW. This provides more flexibility than stems, of course, but it also means that virtually all the mixing remains to be done.

WORKING WITH STEMS

As DAWs became more and more popular, so did the idea of mastering with stems. In the early days, it most likely began with simply two different stems: the instruments and the vocals. This would leave the final say of the all-important vocal/band relationship up to the mastering engineer instead of the mixing engineer. As you may have guessed, people soon began to question the possibility of separating things further.

Today, mastering with stems often involves breaking the song up into one stereo stem for each group of instruments. In a typical session, for example, you may receive the following stems:

- Drums
- Bass
- Guitars
- Keys
- Vocals

Again, each one of these stems would be stereo submixes of several tracks already blended together. So, although the mastering engineer will be able to bring the level of all the guitars up or down, they won't be able to only adjust the level of the acoustic guitar, for example. The same can be said for the individual drum tracks, etc. So why has mastering with stems become a practice? Simply put, it gives the mastering engineer more control. By the same token, it gives the mixing engineer less control, and at some point, a decision needs to be made as to *who* is exactly doing *what*.

If you're considering using a mastering house to master your album, then understand that mastering with stems will no doubt be more costly, as you're asking much more of the mastering engineer. They're not only mastering the album; they're also participating in the mixing process as well. While that may seem like a good idea, considering the fact that they have great ears and usually top-notch rooms, etc., it will certainly be more time-consuming on their end, which results in a larger bill for the customer. Of course, that's not really a consideration if you're mastering your own material. But, again, if it is indeed the case, then you'll most likely be able to fix any serious mix issues by simply doing another mix.

Therefore, mastering with stems is generally something you might want to consider when mastering someone else's work or when you want to shell out some extra money to have a professional master your album.

As for the process, it's very similar in principle to everything we've talked about thus far in the book. The only difference is that you have much more control now than before, as you're able to specifically affect one instrument group at a time. In other words, you'll still be adding a chain of plugins on the master buss as you would in a two-track mastering session, but you'll be able to prepare each individual stem before that stage.

So, for example, if the drums are lacking a bit of excitement, then use a transient designer on them to bring out some attack. If the bass is a bit lackluster, then you can apply any number of harmonic-based plugins—i.e., preamp emulations, etc.—to give it some more weight, etc. If the vocals are sounding slightly shrill, then you can utilize a compressor and/or EQ to tame them, etc. Essentially, you get to make some final mixing decisions before proceeding with the mastering process.

MASTERING SESSION 🔘

Let's close out with a mock mastering session in which we'll aim to make several disparate-sounding tracks sound as though they could coexist on one album without sounding too out of place. As has been noted before, we can't create miracles in the mastering process, and there's no way we can make a track that was recorded during the '90s with a bedroom studio and amateur equipment sound as though it was recorded in a semi-pro studio with expensive gear during the 2010s. But we can do our best to match basic tone, level, and color so that someone won't be constantly reaching for the volume or tone knob on their stereo when listening to the songs back to back.

The first step is to simply take stock of everything you're working with. Generally speaking, it's a good idea to jump into the loudest parts of each track to start with, since we're going to be bringing everything up in the end anyways. So we may as well see what the top level sounds like for each track. Line those spots up and skim through them, making any notes you feel will be helpful at this point. For example, you may have one song that sounds pretty good, which could serve as your reference track for the others. In other words, you'll be trying your best to make all the others match it. If you're not happy with any of the tracks, then you can always pull in a professional track for reference purposes only and aim toward it.

Noting the level and tonal character of each track

Once you have an idea of where you stand and where you'd like to end up—i.e., which track is going to be your benchmark—then it's time to begin the somewhat tedious work of moving song by song and processing each. This means you'll be employing all the techniques you've learned throughout the book to create a sense of cohesion among the tracks. Be sure to watch the accompanying video to see how Michael creatively solves these issues one by one in his mock mastering session.

Organization and Workflow

As opposed to placing each song on its own track at this point, while constantly muting or isolating them any time you move between tracks, it's a lot cleaner if you leave them all on the same track in tandem and automate all your mastering plugins to deal with each song individually. This also allows you to quickly view the settings for any plugin at any point within any song, as the settings on the plugin will change as the cursor is moved from point to point.

CONCLUSION

Congratulations for sticking it out to the end! If you've made it this far and watched all the videos, then you have undoubtedly learned a great deal. But knowledge is only half the battle. Experience is the other half, and that means experimenting with the concepts you've learned. There's simply no substitute for *doing*, and mastering is no different. It's an art in and of itself, just like mixing or playing an instrument. So don't expect to create stellar sounding master tracks right away. While it's true that the tools we have available have created a more level playing field than ever before, they can't do the work for you. The only thing that's going to make you truly good at mastering is to practice it.

To that end, here are some suggestions for getting started in your mastering journeys:

- **Start simple:** In the beginning, try mastering less complex tracks, such as a guitar and vocal only or something similar. This will allow you to get your feet wet without dealing with the complexity of a full band.
- **Try your hand at mastering a friend's album or EP:** The good thing about this is that a friend is likely to be a bit more understanding when you don't exactly hit it out of the park on the first try.
- **Create your own mastering session with recordings of yours that sound very different from one another:** Just as Michael did in the final chapter of this book, do your best to make the tracks sound as cohesive as possible.
- **Experiment with placing your mastering plugins in different orders and listen to the effect:** Place the buss compressor in front of the EQ, and then switch them. Can you hear a difference? What if you use a more extreme setting? Does the difference become more pronounced? Learning the ins and outs of your processing in this manner will allow you to make more informed decisions about what a particular piece of music needs.

Remember to have fun and keep experimenting. Good luck!